**Illinois Central College
Learning Resource Center**

Selected Poems

Robert Hayden

Selected Poems

October House Inc · New York

Acknowledgments

Some of these poems have appeared in the following publications: *American Sampler*, *Atlantic Monthly*, *Beyond the Blues*, *Cross Section 1945*, *ETC.*, *The Fisk Herald*, *Figure of Time*, *The Lion and the Archer*, *The Midwest Journal*, *The Negro Digest*, *Phylon*, *Poetry: A Magazine of Verse*, *The Poetry of the Negro*, *Putting Words in Their Places*, *Soon, One Morning*, *The Tiger's Eye*, *The Twelfth Street Quarterly*, and *Voices*.

The present volume includes poems (several of them in new versions) from *A Ballad of Remembrance*, published in a limited edition by Paul Breman, London.

"O Daedalus, Fly Away Home" was part of a collection in manuscript which won the Hopwood Award for Poetry at the University of Michigan.

Grateful acknowledgment of assistance through grants and fellowships is made to Dr. and Mrs. Theophile Raphael, the Rosenwald Foundation, the Carnegie Foundation, and The Fund for the Advancement of Education.

Published by October House Inc.
55 West 13th Street, New York

For Erma,
again and always,
and for Maia
our daughter

Contents

Three

Four

Five

8

One

The Diver

Sank through easeful
azure. Flower
creatures flashed and
shimmered there—
lost images
fadingly remembered.
Swiftly descended
into canyon of cold
nightgreen emptiness.
Freefalling, weightless
as in dreams of
wingless flight,
plunged through infra-
space and came to
the dead ship,
carcass that swarmed with
voracious life.
Angelfish, their
lively blue and
yellow prised from
darkness by the
flashlight's beam,
thronged her portholes.
Moss of bryozoans
blurred, obscured her
metal. Snappers,
gold groupers explored her,
fearless of bubbling
manfish. I entered
the wreck, awed by her silence,
feeling more keenly
the iron cold.
With flashlight probing
fogs of water
saw the sad slow
dance of gilded
chairs, the ectoplasmic

swirl of garments,
drowned instruments
of buoyancy,
drunken shoes. Then
livid gesturings,
eldritch hide and
seek of laughing
faces. I yearned to
find those hidden
ones, to fling aside
the mask and call to them,
yield to rapturous
whisperings, have
done with self and
every dinning
vain complexity.
Yet in languid
frenzy strove, as
one freezing fights off
sleep desiring sleep;
strove against the
cancelling arms that
suddenly surrounded
me, fled the numbing
kisses that I craved.
Reflex of life-wish?
Respirator's brittle
belling? Swam from
the ship somehow;
somehow began the
measured rise.

Electrical Storm

(for Arna and Alberta)

God's angry with the world again,
the grey neglected ones would say;
He don't like ugly.
Have mercy, Lord, they prayed,
seeing the lightning's
Mene Mene Tekel,
hearing the preaching thunder's deep
Upharsin.
They hunched up, contracting in corners
away from windows and the dog;
huddled under Jehovah's oldtime wrath,
trusting, afraid.

I huddled too, when a boy,
mindful of things they'd told me
God was bound to make me answer for.
But later I was colleged (as they said)
and learned it was not celestial ire
(Beware the infidels, my son)
but pressure systems,
colliding massive energies
that make a storm.
Well for us. . . .

Last night we drove
through suddenly warring weather.
Wind and lightning havocked,
berserked in wires, trees.
Fallen lines we could not see at first
lay in the yard when we reached home.
The hedge was burning in the rain.

Who knows but what
we might have crossed another sill,
had not our neighbors' warning
kept us from our door?
Who knows if it was heavenly design
or chance
(or knows if there's a difference, after all)
that brought us and our neighbors through—
though others died—
the archetypal dangers of the night?

I know what those
cowering true believers would have said.

Full Moon

No longer throne of a goddess to whom we pray,
no longer the bubble house of childhood's
tumbling Mother Goose man,

The emphatic moon ascends—
the brilliant challenger of rocket experts,
the white hope of communications men.

Some I love who are dead
were watchers of the moon and knew its lore;
planted seeds, trimmed their hair,

Pierced their ears for gold hoop earrings
as it waxed or waned.
It shines tonight upon their graves.

And burned in the garden of Gethsemane,
its light made holy by the dazzling tears
with which it mingled.

And spread its radiance on the exile's path
of Him who was The Glorious One,
its light made holy by His holiness.

Already a mooted goal and tomorrow perhaps
an arms base, a livid sector,
the full moon dominates the dark.

Dawnbreaker

Ablaze
with candles sconced
in weeping eyes
    of wounds,

He danced
through jeering streets
to death; oh sang
    against

The drumming
mockery God's praise.
Flames nested in
    his flesh

Fed the
fires that consume
us now, the fire that
    will save.

The Rabbi

Where I grew up, I used to see
the rabbi, dour and pale
in religion's mourner clothes,
walking to the synagogue.

Once there, did he put on
sackcloth and ashes? Wail?
He would not let me in to see
the gold menorah burning.

Mazuzah, Pesach, Chanukah—
these were timbred words I learned,
were things I knew by glimpses.
And I learned schwartze too

And schnapps, which schwartzes bought
on credit from "Jew Baby."
Tippling ironists laughed and said
he'd soon be rich as Rothschild

From their swinish Saturdays.
Hirschel and Molly and I meanwhile
divvied halveh, polly seeds,
were spies and owls and Fu Manchu.

But the synagogue became
New Calvary.
The rabbi bore my friends off
in his prayer shawl.

Belsen, Day of Liberation
(for Rosey)

Her parents and her dolls destroyed,
　　her childhood foreclosed,
she watched the foreign soldiers from
　　the sunlit window whose black bars

Were crooked crosses inked upon
　　her pallid face. "Liebchen,
Liebchen, you should be in bed."
　　But she felt ill no longer.

And because that day was a holy day
　　when even the dead, it seemed,
must rise, she was allowed to stay
　　and see the golden strangers who

Were Father, Brother, and her dream
　　of God. Afterwards
she said, "They were so beautiful,
　　and they were not afraid."

Approximations

i

In dead of winter
wept beside your open grave.
Falling snow.

ii

Darkness, darkness.
I grope and falter. Flare
of a match.

iii

Not sunflowers, not
roses, but rocks in patterned
sand grow here. And bloom.

iv

On the platform at
dawn, grey mailbags waiting;
a crated coffin.

Snow

Smooths and burdens,
endangers, hardens.

Erases, revises.
Extemporizes

Vistas of lunar solitude.
Builds, embellishes a mood.

The Ballad of Sue Ellen Westerfield
(for Clyde)

She grew up in bedeviled southern wilderness,
but had not been a slave, she said,
because her father wept and set her mother free.
She hardened in perilous rivertowns
and after The Surrender,
went as maid upon the tarnished Floating Palaces.
Rivermen reviled her for the rankling cold
sardonic pride
that gave a knife-edge to her comeliness.

When she was old, her back still straight,
her hair still glossy black,
she'd talk sometimes
of dangers lived through on the rivers.
But never told of him,
whose name she'd vowed she would not speak again
till after Jordan.
Oh, he was nearer nearer now
than wearisome kith and kin.
His blue eyes followed her
as she moved about her tasks upon the *Memphis Rose*.
He smiled and joshed, his voice quickening her.
She cursed the circumstance. . . .

The crazing horrors of that summer night,
the swifting flames, he fought his way to her,
the savaging panic, and helped her swim to shore.
The steamer like besieged Atlanta blazing,
the cries, the smoke and bellowing flames,
the flamelit thrashing forms in hellmouth water,
and he swimming out to them,
leaving her dazed and lost.
A woman screaming under the raddled trees—
Sue Ellen felt it was herself who screamed.
The moaning of the hurt, the terrified—
she held off shuddering despair
and went to comfort whom she could.

Wagons torches bells
and whimpering dusk of morning
and blankness lostness nothingness for her
until his arms had lifted her
into wild and secret dark.

How long how long was it they wandered,
loving fearing loving,
fugitives whose dangerous only hidingplace
was love?
How long was it before she knew
she could not forfeit what she was,
even for him—could not, even for him,
forswear her pride?
They kissed and said farewell at last.
He wept as had her father once.
They kissed and said farewell.
Until her dying-bed,
she cursed the circumstance.

Night, Death, Mississippi

I

A quavering cry. Screech-owl?
Or one of them?
The old man in his reek
and gauntness laughs—

One of them, I bet—
and turns out the kitchen lamp,
limping to the porch to listen
in the windowless night.

Be there with Boy and the rest
if I was well again.
Time was. Time was.
White robes like moonlight

In the sweetgum dark.
Unbucked that one then
and him squealing bloody Jesus
as we cut it off.

Time was. A cry?
A cry all right.
He hawks and spits,
fevered as by groinfire.

Have us a bottle,
Boy and me—
he's earned him a bottle—
when he gets home.

II.

Then we beat them, he said,
beat them till our arms was tired

and the big old chains
messy and red.

O Jesus burning on the lily cross

Christ, it was better
than hunting bear
which don't know why
you want him dead.

O night, rawhead and bloodybones night

You kids fetch Paw
some water now so's he
can wash that blood
off him, she said.

O night betrayed by darkness not its own

Two

"An Inference of Mexico"
(*for Hank and Richard*)

Day of the Dead

(*Tehuantepec*)

The vultures hover wheel and hover
in skies intense as voyeur's gazing.

Cruciform black bells of clay
serenade Mr. and Mrs. Death
exposed in wedding clothes.

    Savage the light upon us,
    savage the light.

The graveblack vultures encircle afternoon,
transformed by steeps of flight
into dark pure images of flight.

    Such pretty girls in Juchitán, señor,
    and if one desires—

Death brings an almond sweetness
to the lips of children playing
with Jack-in-the-tomb and skulls of marzipan.

The tilting vultures glide
through causeway smoke to carrion.

In flowered shirt, androgynous,
the young man under palmleaf knives of sunlight
invites, awaits, obliquely smiles.

    Such pretty girls, señor,
    but if instead—

Barefoot Tehuanas in rhythmic jewels of gold
bear pails of marigolds upon their heads
to the returning dead.

    Flee, amigo, for the dead are angry;
    flee, lest the hands of dead men strike us down,

    and the vultures pick our bones.

Mountains

Dark as if cloven from darkness
were those mountains.

Night-angled fold on fold
they rose in mist and sunlight,

Their surging darkness
drums bells gongs imploring a god.

Veracruz

Sunday afternoon,
and couples walk the breakwater
heedless of the bickering spray.
Near the shoreward end,
Indian boys idle and fish.
A shawled brown woman
squinting against
the ricocheting brilliance
of sun and water
shades her eyes and gazes
toward the fort,
fossil of Spanish power,
looming in the harbor.

At the seaward end,
a pharos like a temple rises.
From here the shore
seen across marbling waves
is arabesque ornately green
that hides the inward-falling slum,
the stains and dirty tools of struggle;
appears a destination dreamed of,
never to be reached.

Here only the sea is real—
the barbarous multifoliate sea
with its rustling of leaves,
fire, garments, wind;
its clashing of phantasmal jewels,
its lunar thunder,
animal and human sighing.

Leap now
and cease from error.
Escape. Or shoreward turn,

accepting all—
the losses and farewells,
the long warfare with self,
with God.

The waves roar in and break
roar in and break
with granite spreeing hiss
on bronzegreen rocks below
and glistering upfling of spray.

II.

Thus reality
   bedizened in the warring colors
     of a dream
parades through these
   arcades ornate with music and
     the sea.

Thus reality
   become unbearably a dream
     beckons
out of reach in flyblown streets
   of lapsing rose and purple, dying
     blue.

Thus marimba'd night
   and multifoliate sea become
     phantasmal
space, and there,
   light-years away, one farewell image
     burns and fades and burns.

Idol

(Coatlicue, Aztec goddess)

Wail of the newborn, cry of the dying,
sirenscream of agonies;
taloned shriek, gong and cymbal of wreckage,
drumbeat of bloodblackened praise;
soundless drumthrob of the heart wrenched
from the living breast,
of the raw meaty heart quivering in copal
smoke its praise.

Sub Specie Aeternitatis

High amid
gothic rocks the altar stands
that honored once
    a tippling fiercely joyous god.
    Far below,
the empty convent lifts
its cross against a dark
    invasive as the sun
    whose plangent fire
moves like feathered snakes
in trees that shade
    the cloister-garth.

The curious
may walk the cloister now,
may enter portals barred
    to them no longer
    and wander
hidden passageways and rooms
of stone, meditating on
    such gods as they possess,
    as they have lost.

Hollow cells
are desolate in their
tranquility
    as relic skulls.
    Arched windows there
look toward the firegreen mountain
resonant with silence of
    a conquered and
    defiant god.

Market

Ragged boys
lift sweets, haggle
for acid-green
and bloody gelatins.
A broken smile
dandles its weedy
cigarette
over papayas too ripe
and pyramids
of rotting oranges.
Turkeys like feather-
duster flowers
lie trussed in bunchy smother.
The barefoot cripple
foraging crawls
among rinds, orts,
chewed butts, trampled
peony droppings—
his hunger litany
and suppliant before
altars of mamey,
pineapple, mango.
Turistas pass.
Por caridad, por caridad.
Lord, how they stride
on the hard good legs
money has made them.
Ay! you creatures
who have walked
on seas of money all
your foreign lives!
Por caridad.
Odor of a dripping
carcass moans
beneath the hot
fragrance of carnations,
cool scent of lilies.

Starveling dogs
hover in the reek
of frying; ashy feet
(the twistfoot beggar laughs)
kick at them in vain.
Aloft, the Fire King's
flashing mask of tin
looks down with eyes
of sunstruck glass.

Kid

(Cuernavaca)

He is found with the homeless dogs
    that worry sidewalk cafes
where gringos in dollar bills
    deplore and sip. He has

Tricks of pathos for
    the silly foreigners
and so manages not to starve.
    Waiters strike at him and curse;

Deft and quick and accustomed,
    he dances beyond their blows,
taunts them and scampers off,
    laughing as he goes.

La Corrida

I. *El toro*

From the blind kingdom
where his horns are law,

Gigantically plunging and charging,
he enters the clockface labyrinth—

Man-in-beast, creature
whose guileless power is his doom.

II. *El matador*

In the heart of the maze
whose ritual pathways
goading lance, bloodflowering dart,
veronica and sword define,

The fateful one, fate's dazzler,
gleams in suit of lights,
prepares for sensual death
his moment of mocking truth.

In the fiery heart of the maze
the bullgod moves,
transfiguring death
and the wish to die.

III. *Sol y sombra*

From all we are yet cannot be
deliver, oh redeem us now.

Of all we know and do not wish
to know, purge oh purge us now.

Olé!

Upon the cross of horns
be crucified for us.

Die for us that death
may call us back to life.

Olé!

Three

A Ballad of Remembrance

Quadroon mermaids, Afro angels, black saints
balanced upon the switchblades of that air
and sang. Tight streets unfolding to the eye
like fans of corrosion and elegiac lace
crackled with their singing: Shadow of time. Shadow of blood.

Shadow, echoed the Zulu king, dangling
from a cluster of balloons. Blood,
whined the gun-metal priestess, floating
over the courtyard where dead men diced.

What will you have? she inquired, the sallow vendeuse
of prepared tarnishes and jokes of nacre and ormolu,
what but those gleamings, oldrose graces,
manners like scented gloves? Contrived ghosts
rapped to metronome clack of lavalieres.

Contrived illuminations riding a threat
of river, masked Negroes wearing chameleon
satins gaudy now as a fortuneteller's
dream of disaster, lighted the crazy flopping
dance of love and hate among joys, rejections.

Accommodate, muttered the Zulu king,
toad on a throne of glaucous poison jewels.
Love, chimed the saints and the angels and the mermaids.
Hate, shrieked the gun-metal priestess
from her spiked bellcollar curved like a fleur-de-lis:

As well have a talon as a finger, a muzzle as a mouth,
as well have a hollow as a heart. And she pinwheeled
away in coruscations of laughter, scattering
those others before her like foil stars.

But the dance continued—now among metaphorical
doors, coffee cups floating poised
hysterias, decors of illusion; now among
mazurka dolls offering death's-heads
of cocaine roses and real violets.

Then you arrived, meditative, ironic,
richly human; and your presence was shore where I rested
released from the hoodoo of that dance, where I spoke
with my true voice again.

And therefore this is not only a ballad of remembrance
for the down-South arcane city with death
in its jaws like gold teeth and archaic cusswords;
not only a token for the troubled generous friends
held in the fists of that schizoid city like flowers,
but also, Mark Van Doren,
a poem of remembrance, a gift, a souvenir for you.

Tour 5

The road winds down through autumn hills
in blazonry of farewell scarlet
and recessional gold,
past cedar groves, through static villages
whose names are all that's left
of Choctaw, Chickasaw.

We stop a moment in a town
watched over by Confederate sentinels,
buy gas and ask directions of a rawboned man
whose eyes revile us as the enemy.

Shrill gorgon silence breathes behind
his taut civility
and in the ever-tautening air,
dark for us despite its Indian summer glow.
We drive on, following the route
of highwaymen and phantoms,

Of slaves and armies.
Children, wordless and remote,
wave at us from kindling porches.
And now the land is flat for miles,
the landscape lush, metallic, flayed,
its brightness harsh as bloodstained swords.

Gulls

In sun-whetted
      morning,
the dropped gull
      splayed
on sand,
      wind
picking at
      its feathers.

Over the headlong
      toppling
rush and leashed-back
      mica'd
fall of the sea,
      gulls
scouting and
      crying.

A Road in Kentucky

And when that ballad lady went
    to ease the lover whose life she broke,
oh surely this is the road she took,
    road all hackled through barberry fire,
through cedar and alder and sumac and thorn.

Red clay stained her flounces
    and stones cut her shoes
and the road twisted on to his loveless house
    and his cornfield dying
in the scarecrow's arms.

And when she had left her lover lying
    so stark and so stark, with the Star-of-Hope
drawn over his eyes, oh this is the road
    that lady walked in the cawing light,
so dark and so dark in the briary light.

Homage to the Empress of the Blues

Because there was a man somewhere in a candystripe silk shirt,
gracile and dangerous as a jaguar and because a woman moaned
for him in sixty-watt gloom and mourned him Faithless Love
Twotiming Love Oh Love Oh Careless Aggravating Love,

> She came out on the stage in yards of pearls, emerging like
> a favorite scenic view, flashed her golden smile and sang.

Because grey laths began somewhere to show from underneath
torn hurdygurdy lithographs of dollfaced heaven;
and because there were those who feared alarming fists of snow
on the door and those who feared the riot-squad of statistics,

> She came out on the stage in ostrich feathers, beaded satin,
> and shone that smile on us and sang.

"The Burly Fading One"

The burly fading one beside the engine,
holding a lantern in his hand,
is Uncle Jed—bullyboy
of wintered recollections now.

Coal miner, stevedore and railroad man,
oh how he brawls and loves,
a Bible over his headlong heart
and no liquor on his breath.

And when he dies, dies not in his own
well-mastered bed but in the waters
of the Johnstown flood, in wild attempt—
so sibling innuendoes all aver—

To save the jolly girl
his wife had mortally wished dead.

"Incense of the Lucky Virgin"

Incense of the Lucky Virgin,
High John the Conqueror
didn't bring him home again,
didn't get his children fed,
    get his children fed.

I prayed and what did prayer avail?
My candles held no power.
An evening came I prayed no more
and blew my candles out,
    oh blew my candles out.

Put on your Sunday ribbon-bows,
Cleola, Willie Mae;
you, Garland, go
and shine your Sunday shoes,
    make haste and shine your shoes.

They were so happy they forgot
they were hungry, daddyless.
Except Cleola maybe—she
wasn't asking, Where we going,
    Mommy, where we going?

Garland was too quick for me
(he didn't yell once as he ran);
Cleola, Willie Mae
won't be hungry any more,
    oh they'll never cry and hunger any more.

Witch Doctor

I.

He dines alone surrounded by reflections
of himself. Then after sleep and benzedrine
descends the Cinquecento stair his magic
wrought from hypochondria of the well-
to-do and nagging deathwish of the poor;
swirls on smiling genuflections of
his liveried chauffeur into a crested
lilac limousine, the cynosure
of mousey neighbors tittering behind
Venetian blinds and half afraid of him
and half admiring his outrageous flair.

II.

Meanwhile his mother, priestess in gold lamé,
precedes him to the quondam theater
now Israel Temple of the Highest Alpha,
where the bored, the sick, the alien, the tired
await euphoria. With deadly vigor
she prepares the way for mystery
and lucre. Shouts in blues-contralto, "He's
God's dictaphone of all-redeeming truth.
Oh he's the holyweight champeen who's come
to give the knockout lick to your bad luck;
say he's the holyweight champeen who's here
to deal a knockout punch to your hard luck."

III.

Reposing on cushions of black leopard skin,
he telephones instructions for a long
slow drive across the park that burgeons now
with spring and sailors. Peers questingly
into the green fountainous twilight, sighs
and turns the gold-plate dial to Music For
Your Dining-Dancing Pleasure. Smoking Egyptian
cigarettes rehearses in his mind
a new device that he must use tonight.

IV.

Approaching Israel Temple, mask in place,
he hears ragtime allegros of a "Song
of Zion" that becomes when he appears
a hallelujah wave for him to walk.
His mother and a rainbow-surpliced cordon
conduct him choiring to the altar-stage,
and there he kneels and seems to pray before
a lighted Jesus painted sealskin-brown.
Then with a glittering flourish he arises,
turns, gracefully extends his draperied arms:
"Israelites, true Jews, O found lost tribe
of Israel, receive my blessing now.
Selah, selah." He feels them yearn toward him
as toward a lover, exults before the image
of himself their trust gives back. Stands as though
in meditation, letting their eyes caress
his garments jewelled and chatoyant, cut
to fall, to flow from his tall figure
dramatically just so. Then all at once
he sways, quivers, gesticulates as if
to ward off blows or kisses, and when he speaks
again he utters wildering vocables,
hypnotic no-words planned (and never failing)
to enmesh his flock in theopathic tension.
Cries of eudaemonic pain attest
his artistry. Behind the mask he smiles.
And now in subtly altering light he chants
and sinuously trembles, chants and trembles
while convulsive energies of eager faith
surcharge the theater with power of
their own, a power he has counted on
and for a space allows to carry him.
Dishevelled antiphons proclaim the moment
his followers all day have hungered for,
but which is his alone.
He signals: tambourines begin, frenetic

drumbeat and glissando. He dances from the altar,
robes hissing, flaring, shimmering; down aisles
where mantled guardsmen intercept wild hands
that arduously strain to clutch his vestments,
he dances, dances, ensorcelled and aloof,
the fervid juba of God as lover, healer,
conjurer. And of himself as God.

Mourning Poem for the Queen of Sunday

Lord's lost Him His mockingbird,
His fancy warbler;
Satan sweet-talked her,
four bullets hushed her.
Who would have thought
she'd end that way?

Four bullets hushed her. And the world a-clang with evil.
Who's going to make old hardened sinner men tremble now
and the righteous rock?
Oh who and oh who will sing Jesus down
to help with struggling and doing without and being colored
all through blue Monday?
Till way next Sunday?

All those angels
in their cretonne clouds and finery
the true believer saw
when she rared back her head and sang,
all those angels are surely weeping.
Who would have thought
she'd end that way?

Four holes in her heart. The gold works wrecked.
But she looks so natural in her big bronze coffin
among the Broken Hearts and Gates-Ajar,
it's as if any moment she'd lift her head
from its pillow of chill gardenias
and turn this quiet into shouting Sunday
and make folks forget what she did on Monday.

Oh, Satan sweet-talked her,
and four bullets hushed her.
Lord's lost Him His diva,
His fancy warbler's gone.
Who would have thought,
who would have thought she'd end that way?

Four

"Summertime and the Living . . ."

Nobody planted roses, he recalls,
but sunflowers gangled there sometimes,
tough-stalked and bold
and like the vivid children there unplanned.
There circus-poster horses curveted
in trees of heaven
above the quarrels and shattered glass,
and he was bareback rider of them all.

No roses there in summer—
oh, never roses except when people died—
and no vacations for his elders,
so harshened after each unrelenting day
that they were shouting-angry.
But summer was, they said, the poor folks' time
of year. And he remembers
how they would sit on broken steps amid

The fevered tossings of the dusk, the dark,
wafting hearsay with funeral-parlor fans
or making evening solemn by
their quietness. Feels their Mosaic eyes
upon him, though the florist roses
that only sorrow could afford
long since have bidden them Godspeed.

Oh, summer summer summertime—

Then grim street preachers shook
their tambourines and Bibles in the face
of tolerant wickedness;
then Elks parades and big splendiferous
Jack Johnson in his diamond limousine
set the ghetto burgeoning
with fantasies
of Ethiopia spreading her gorgeous wings.

The Whipping

The old woman across the way
      is whipping the boy again
and shouting to the neighborhood
      her goodness and his wrongs.

Wildly he crashes through elephant ears,
      pleads in dusty zinnias,
while she in spite of crippling fat
      pursues and corners him.

She strikes and strikes the shrilly circling
      boy till the stick breaks
in her hand. His tears are rainy weather
      to woundlike memories:

My head gripped in bony vise
      of knees, the writhing struggle
to wrench free, the blows, the fear
      worse than blows that hateful

Words could bring, the face that I
      no longer knew or loved . . .
Well, it is over now, it is over,
      and the boy sobs in his room,

And the woman leans muttering against
      a tree, exhausted, purged—
avenged in part for lifelong hidings
      she has had to bear.

Those Winter Sundays

Sundays too my father got up early
and put his clothes on in the blueblack cold,
then with cracked hands that ached
from labor in the weekday weather made
banked fires blaze. No one ever thanked him.

I'd wake and hear the cold splintering, breaking.
When the rooms were warm, he'd call,
and slowly I would rise and dress,
fearing the chronic angers of that house,

Speaking indifferently to him,
who had driven out the cold
and polished my good shoes as well.
What did I know, what did I know
of love's austere and lonely offices?

The Web

My hand by chance
brushed and tore
a spider's web;

The spider dangled,
aerialist hanging
by a thread,

Then fled the ruin,
fit snare for nothing
now but my

Embittered thoughts
of a web
more intricate,

More fragile—and
the stronger for
its fragileness.

Its iron gossamer
withstands the blows
that would destroy.

Caught in that filmy
trap, who shall
contrive escape?

The Wheel

Gentle and smiling as before,
he stroked the leopard purring by his chair
and whispered silkily to me.
And though I knew he lied,
lied with every flicker of
his jewelled hands,

I listened and believed,
persuaded as before
by what he seemed to say
yet did not say.
And when, face close to mine,
he murmured that equivocal command,

I went to do his bidding as before.
And so once more,
the useless errand bitterly accomplished,
I crouch in the foulness of a ditch;
like traitor, thief or murderer hide
and curse the moon and fear the rising of the sun.

Perseus

Her sleeping head with its great gelid mass
    of serpents torpidly astir
burned into the mirroring shield—
    a scathing image dire
as hated truth the mind accepts at last
    and festers on.
I struck. The shield flashed bare.

Yet even as I lifted up the head
    and started from that place
of gazing silences and terrored stone,
    I thirsted to destroy.
None could have passed me then—
    no garland-bearing girl, no priest
or staring boy—and lived.

Theme and Variation

I.

Fossil, fuschia, mantis, man,
fire and water, earth and air—
all things alter even as I behold,
all things alter, the stranger said.

Alter, become a something more,
a something less. Are the revelling shadows
of a changing permanence. Are, are not
and same and other, the stranger said.

II.

I sense, he said, the lurking rush, the sly
transience flickering at the edge of things.
I've spied from the corner of my eye
upon the striptease of reality.

There is, there is, he said, an imminence
that turns to curiosa all I know;
that changes light to rainbow darkness
wherein God waylays us and empowers.

"From the Corpse Woodpiles, From the Ashes"

From the corpse woodpiles, from the ashes
and staring pits of Dachau,
Buchenwald they come—

O David, Hirschel, Eva,
cops and robbers with me once,
their faces are like yours—

From Johannesburg, from Seoul.
Their struggles are all horizons.
Their deaths encircle me.

Through target streets I run,
in light part nightmare
and part vision fleeing

What I cannot flee, and reach
that cold cloacal cell
where He, who is man beatified

And Godly mystery,
lies chained, His pain
our anguish and our anodyne.

Bahá'u'lláh in the Garden of Ridwan

Agonies confirm His hour,
  and swords like compass-needles turn
    toward His heart.

The midnight air is forested
  with presences that shelter Him
    and sheltering praise

The auroral darkness which is God
  and sing the word made flesh again
    in Him,

Eternal exile whose return
  epiphanies repeatedly
    foretell.

He watches in a borrowed garden,
  prays. And sleepers toss upon
    their armored beds,

Half-roused by golden knocking at
  the doors of consciousness. Energies
    like angels dance

Glorias of recognition.
  Within the rock the undiscovered suns
    release their light.

Five

Middle Passage

I.

Jesús, Estrella, Esperanza, Mercy:

> Sails flashing to the wind like weapons,
> sharks following the moans the fever and the dying;
> horror the corposant and compass rose.

Middle Passage:
>> voyage through death
>>> to life upon these shores.

> "10 April 1800—
> Blacks rebellious. Crew uneasy. Our linguist says
> their moaning is a prayer for death,
> ours and their own. Some try to starve themselves.
> Lost three this morning leaped with crazy laughter
> to the waiting sharks, sang as they went under."

Desire, Adventure, Tartar, Ann:

> Standing to America, bringing home
> black gold, black ivory, black seed.

>> *Deep in the festering hold thy father lies,*
>> *of his bones New England pews are made,*
>> *those are altar lights that were his eyes.*

Jesus Saviour Pilot Me
Over Life's Tempestuous Sea

We pray that Thou wilt grant, O Lord,
safe passage to our vessels bringing
heathen souls unto Thy chastening.

Jesus Saviour

"8 bells. I cannot sleep, for I am sick
with fear, but writing eases fear a little
since still my eyes can see these words take shape
upon the page & so I write, as one
would turn to exorcism. 4 days scudding,
but now the sea is calm again. Misfortune
follows in our wake like sharks (our grinning
tutelary gods). Which one of us
has killed an albatross? A plague among
our blacks—Ophthalmia: blindness—& we
have jettisoned the blind to no avail.
It spreads, the terrifying sickness spreads.
Its claws have scratched sight from the Capt.'s eyes
& there is blindness in the fo'c'sle
& we must sail 3 weeks before we come
to port."

> *What port awaits us, Davy Jones'*
> *or home? I've heard of slavers drifting, drifting,*
> *playthings of wind and storm and chance, their crews*
> *gone blind, the jungle hatred*
> *crawling up on deck.*

Thou Who Walked On Galilee

"Deponent further sayeth *The Bella J*
left the Guinea Coast
with cargo of five hundred blacks and odd
for the barracoons of Florida:

"That there was hardly room 'tween-decks for half
the sweltering cattle stowed spoon-fashion there;
that some went mad of thirst and tore their flesh
and sucked the blood:

"That Crew and Captain lusted with the comeliest
of the savage girls kept naked in the cabins;

66

that there was one they called The Guinea Rose
and they cast lots and fought to lie with her:

"That when the Bo's'n piped all hands, the flames
spreading from starboard already were beyond
control, the negroes howling and their chains
entangled with the flames:

"That the burning blacks could not be reached,
that the Crew abandoned ship,
leaving their shrieking negresses behind,
that the Captain perished drunken with the wenches:

"Further Deponent sayeth not."

Pilot Oh Pilot Me

II.

Aye, lad, and I have seen those factories,
Gambia, Rio Pongo, Calabar;
have watched the artful mongos baiting traps
of war wherein the victor and the vanquished

Were caught as prizes for our barracoons.
Have seen the nigger kings whose vanity
and greed turned wild black hides of Fellatah,
Mandingo, Ibo, Kru to gold for us.

And there was one—King Anthracite we named him—
fetish face beneath French parasols
of brass and orange velvet, impudent mouth
whose cups were carven skulls of enemies:

He'd honor us with drum and feast and conjo
and palm-oil-glistening wenches deft in love,

and for tin crowns that shone with paste,
red calico and German-silver trinkets

Would have the drums talk war and send
his warriors to burn the sleeping villages
and kill the sick and old and lead the young
in coffles to our factories.

Twenty years a trader, twenty years,
for there was wealth aplenty to be harvested
from those black fields, and I'd be trading still
but for the fevers melting down my bones.

III.

Shuttles in the rocking loom of history,
the dark ships move, the dark ships move,
their bright ironical names
like jests of kindness on a murderer's mouth;
plough through thrashing glister toward
fata morgana's lucent melting shore,
weave toward New World littorals that are
mirage and myth and actual shore.

Voyage through death,
      voyage whose chartings are unlove.

A charnel stench, effluvium of living death
spreads outward from the hold,
where the living and the dead, the horribly dying,
lie interlocked, lie foul with blood and excrement.

> *Deep in the festering hold thy father lies,*
> *the corpse of mercy rots with him,*
> *rats eat love's rotten gelid eyes.*
>
> *But, oh, the living look at you*
> *with human eyes whose suffering accuses you,*

whose hatred reaches through the swill of dark
to strike you like a leper's claw.

You cannot stare that hatred down
or chain the fear that stalks the watches
and breathes on you its fetid scorching breath;
cannot kill the deep immortal human wish,
the timeless will.

"But for the storm that flung up barriers
of wind and wave, *The Amistad*, señores,
would have reached the port of Príncipe in two,
three days at most; but for the storm we should
have been prepared for what befell.
Swift as the puma's leap it came. There was
that interval of moonless calm filled only
with the water's and the rigging's usual sounds,
then sudden movement, blows and snarling cries
and they had fallen on us with machete
and marlinspike. It was as though the very
air, the night itself were striking us.
Exhausted by the rigors of the storm,
we were no match for them. Our men went down
before the murderous Africans. Our loyal
Celestino ran from below with gun
and lantern and I saw, before the cane-
knife's wounding flash, Cinquez,
that surly brute who calls himself a prince,
directing, urging on the ghastly work.
He hacked the poor mulatto down, and then
he turned on me. The decks were slippery
when daylight finally came. It sickens me
to think of what I saw, of how these apes
threw overboard the butchered bodies of
our men, true Christians all, like so much jetsam.
Enough, enough. The rest is quickly told:
Cinquez was forced to spare the two of us

69

you see to steer the ship to Africa,
and we like phantoms doomed to rove the sea
voyaged east by day and west by night,
deceiving them, hoping for rescue,
prisoners on our own vessel, till
at length we drifted to the shores of this
your land, America, where we were freed
from our unspeakable misery. Now we
demand, good sirs, the extradition of
Cinquez and his accomplices to La
Havana. And it distresses us to know
there are so many here who seem inclined
to justify the mutiny of these blacks.
We find it paradoxical indeed
that you whose wealth, whose tree of liberty
are rooted in the labor of your slaves
should suffer the august John Quincy Adams
to speak with so much passion of the right
of chattel slaves to kill their lawful masters
and with his Roman rhetoric weave a hero's
garland for Cinquez. I tell you that
we are determined to return to Cuba
with our slaves and there see justice done. Cinquez—
or let us say 'the Prince'—Cinquez shall die."

The deep immortal human wish,
the timeless will:

      Cinquez its deathless primaveral image,
      life that transfigures many lives.

Voyage through death
                to life upon these shores.

O Daedalus, Fly Away Home

Drifting night in the Georgia pines,
coonskin drum and jubilee banjo.
    Pretty Malinda, dance with me.

Night is juba, night is conjo.
    Pretty Malinda, dance with me.

Night is an African juju man
weaving a wish and a weariness together
    to make two wings.

    O fly away home fly away

Do you remember Africa?

    O cleave the air fly away home

My gran, he flew back to Africa,
just spread his arms and
    flew away home.

Drifting night in the windy pines;
night is a laughing, night is a longing.
    Pretty Malinda, come to me.

Night is a mourning juju man
weaving a wish and a weariness together
    to make two wings.

    O fly away home fly away

The Ballad of Nat Turner

Then fled, O brethren, the wicked juba
    and wandered wandered far
from curfew joys in the Dismal's night.
    Fool of St. Elmo's fire

In scary night I wandered, praying,
    Lord God my harshener,
speak to me now or let me die;
    speak, Lord, to this mourner.

And came at length to livid trees
    where Ibo warriors
hung shadowless, turning in wind
    that moaned like Africa,

Their belltongue bodies dead, their eyes
    alive with the anger deep
in my own heart. Is this the sign,
    the sign forepromised me?

The spirits vanished. Afraid and lonely
    I wandered on in blackness.
Speak to me now or let me die.
    Die, whispered the blackness.

And wild things gasped and scuffled in
    the night; seething shapes
of evil frolicked upon the air.
    I reeled with fear, I prayed.

Sudden brightness clove the preying
    darkness, brightness that was
itself a golden darkness, brightness
    so bright that it was darkness.

And there were angels, their faces hidden
    from me, angels at war

with one another, angels in dazzling
        combat. And oh the splendor,

The fearful splendor of that warring.
        Hide me, I cried to rock and bramble.
Hide me, the rock, the bramble cried. . . .
        How tell you of that holy battle?

The shock of wing on wing and sword
        on sword was the tumult of
a taken city burning. I cannot
        say how long they strove,

For the wheel in a turning wheel which is time
        in eternity had ceased
its whirling, and owl and moccasin,
        panther and nameless beast

And I were held like creatures fixed
        in flaming, in fiery amber.
But I saw I saw oh many of
        those mighty beings waver,

Waver and fall, go streaking down
        into swamp water, and the water
hissed and steamed and bubbled and locked
        shuddering shuddering over

The fallen and soon was motionless.
        Then that massive light
began a-folding slowly in
        upon itself, and I

Beheld the conqueror faces and, lo,
        they were like mine, I saw
they were like mine and in joy and terror
        wept, praising praising Jehovah.

Oh praised my honer, harshener
        till a sleep came over me,
a sleep heavy as death. And when
        I awoke at last free

And purified, I rose and prayed
        and returned after a time
to the blazing fields, to the humbleness.
        And bided my time.

Runagate Runagate

Runs falls rises stumbles on from darkness into darkness
and the darkness thicketed with shapes of terror
and the hunters pursuing and the hounds pursuing
and the night cold and the night long and the river
to cross and the jack-muh-lanterns beckoning beckoning
and blackness ahead and when shall I reach that somewhere
morning and keep on going and never turn back and keep on going

    Runagate
      Runagate
        Runagate

Many thousands rise and go
many thousands crossing over

          O mythic North
        O star-shaped yonder Bible city

Some go weeping and some rejoicing
some in coffins and some in carriages
some in silks and some in shackles

    Rise and go or fare you well

No more auction block for me
no more driver's lash for me

    If you see my Pompey, 30 yrs of age,
    new breeches, plain stockings, negro shoes;
    if you see my Anna, likely young mulatto
    branded E on the right cheek, R on the left,
    catch them if you can and notify subscriber.
    Catch them if you can, but it won't be easy.
    They'll dart underground when you try to catch them,
    plunge into quicksand, whirlpools, mazes,
    turn into scorpions when you try to catch them.

And before I'll be a slave
I'll be buried in my grave

> North star and bonanza gold
> I'm bound for the freedom, freedom-bound
> and oh Susyanna don't you cry for me

> Runagate

> Runagate

II.

Rises from their anguish and their power,

> Harriet Tubman,

> woman of earth, whipscarred,
> a summoning, a shining

> Mean to be free

And this was the way of it, brethren brethren,
way we journeyed from Can't to Can.
Moon so bright and no place to hide,
the cry up and the patterollers riding,
hound dogs belling in bladed air.
And fear starts a-murbling, Never make it,
we'll never make it. *Hush that now*,
and she's turned upon us, levelled pistol
glinting in the moonlight:
Dead folks can't jaybird-talk, she says;
you keep on going now or die, she says.

Wanted   Harriet Tubman   alias The General
alias Moses   Stealer of Slaves

In league with Garrison   Alcott   Emerson
Garrett   Douglass   Thoreau   John Brown

Armed and known to be Dangerous

Wanted   Reward   Dead or Alive

    Tell me, Ezekiel, oh tell me do you see
    mailed Jehovah coming to deliver me?

Hoot-owl calling in the ghosted air,
five times calling to the hants in the air.
Shadow of a face in the scary leaves,
shadow of a voice in the talking leaves:

    Come ride-a my train

    Oh that train, ghost-story train
    through swamp and savanna movering movering,
    over trestles of dew, through caves of the wish,
    Midnight Special on a sabre track movering movering,
    first stop Mercy and the last Hallelujah.

    Come ride-a my train

      Mean mean mean to be free.

Frederick Douglass

When it is finally ours, this freedom, this liberty, this beautiful
and terrible thing, needful to man as air,
usable as earth; when it belongs at last to all,
when it is truly instinct, brain matter, diastole, systole,
reflex action; when it is finally won; when it is more
than the gaudy mumbo jumbo of politicians:
this man, this Douglass, this former slave, this Negro
beaten to his knees, exiled, visioning a world
where none is lonely, none hunted, alien,
this man, superb in love and logic, this man
shall be remembered. Oh, not with statues' rhetoric,
not with legends and poems and wreaths of bronze alone,
but with the lives grown out of his life, the lives
fleshing his dream of the beautiful, needful thing.

Notes to Poems

Full Moon
The Glorious One: One of the titles given to Bahá'u'lláh, prophet of the Baha'i faith.

Dawnbreaker
"Dawnbreakers" is the title now used to designate the early Persian Baha'is, thousands of whom were martyred.

Incense of the Lucky Virgin
High John the Conqueror: A root said to have magical properties, used by conjurers.

"From the Corpse Woodpiles, From the Ashes"
He, who is man beatified: Bahá'u'lláh was imprisoned as a heretic in 1853.

Bahá'u'lláh in the Garden of Ridwan
He declared His mission in the Garden of Ridwan while on His way to prison and exile in 1863.

Middle Passage
Part Three follows, in the main, the account of the *Amistad* mutiny given by Muriel Rukeyser in her biography of Willard Gibbs.

The Ballad of Nat Turner
Nat Turner led a slave revolt in Jerusalem, Virginia in 1831.